Original title:
Life's Purpose: A Riddle Wrapped in a Mystery

Copyright © 2025 Creative Arts Management OÜ
All rights reserved.

Author: Riley Donovan
ISBN HARDBACK: 978-1-80566-065-1
ISBN PAPERBACK: 978-1-80566-360-7

The Canvas of Choice

A jester holds a brush so bright,
Painting dreams beneath the light.
He mixes colors, giggles too,
What shall I paint? A cow in a shoe?

The canvas stretches, wide and free,
Shall I draw a cat that sings off key?
Or maybe a dog with a top hat bold,
Listening to tales that never get old.

Each stroke a puzzle, a twist, a turn,
Tickles the mind, makes the stomach churn.
An octopus dances, a fish wears a crown,
Chasing its tail, while wearing a frown.

Questions like confetti, scattered about,
What's this nonsense? Can it be stout?
A squirrel with glasses, pondering fate,
Is it too silly, or just first-rate?

The laughter echoes, a joyous spree,
In the art of the whimsy, we all just agree.
That in every stroke, a chuckle ignites,
Creating a canvas of giggles and lights.

What Lies Beneath

In shadows deep, we often stare,
At socks that hide, just under there.
The missing mate, a puzzling plight,
Is it a ghost or just the night?

The cat's on guard, with eyes so wide,
What secrets dwell when dogs collide?
Is wisdom found in a rubber shoe?
Or do you just need to look askew?

The Search for Clarity

I grasped a thought, it slipped away,
Like buttered toast on a rainy day.
The distant echoes of what could be,
Are they just echoes, or a lost decree?

I chased my tail, round and round,
A circus act on shaky ground.
The Clarity Monster, quite a tease,
Hiding behind my own shenanigans, with ease!

The Unwritten Scroll

A scroll of dreams, so blank, so wide,
My plans turned out to take a ride.
With crayons and giggles, I drew a cow,
Who said, 'That's deep!' but also, 'Wow!'

An epic tale of jellybeans,
With heroes clad in silly jeans.
Each scribble bold, absurd, and bright,
The unwritten scroll is pure delight!

Whirls of Wonder

In a whirlwind spin, on a roller chair,
I wondered where my snack had gone somewhere.
Around I twirled, searching for the pie,
It vanished, poof! Like a brave goodbye.

Confetti thoughts, they're hard to catch,
A mix of logic, humor, and a scratch.
With every spin, I giggle loud,
Oh, mysteries lurk in the funniest crowd!

Shadows of Desire

In the shadow of my dreams, I tiptoe,
Chasing whims like a three-legged crow,
With snacks on my mind and a jig in my stride,
I ponder the reason I'm here, what a ride!

Do ducks get a purpose, or just waddle around?
While squirrels plot heists for the lost acorn mound.
In this circus of beings, with antics so grand,
I laugh at the puzzle, that's life on demand.

The Enigma of Being

Tickling my chin, I ponder and spout,
Why do my socks go missing? What's that about?
I chase the odd rabbit down into a hole,
Reflecting on questions that scramble my soul.

Is the cat really plotting my next meal with flair?
Or lounging with purpose, like it just doesn't care?
In the circus of chaos, hilarity reigns,
As I dig for the answers, with laughter and pains.

Threads of Destiny

Life's like a sweater with holes and some frays,
Each thread tells a story in mysterious ways.
With mismatched buttons and sleeves full of cheer,
I unravel the knitting while drinking my beer.

The fate of my laundry? It's anyone's guess,
Will the red sock turn white? Oh, what a mess!
Yet here in this yarn, I find joy in the knits,
While searching for meaning in laundry room wit.

Clues Within the Chaos

Amidst all this clutter, I find my lost shoe,
A riddle of sorts that my brain can't construe.
A T-Rex on my shirt and my dog wears a hat,
Searching for wisdom in a world that's a cat.

The crumbs from my snack are a treasure map fine,
Leading me to answers in pizza-shaped lines.
With giggles and wiggles, I float like a breeze,
Finding my meaning in life's playful tease.

Patterns in the Chaos

In a world of tangled thread,
The sock's on the cat instead.
The coffee spills, the toast will burn,
Yet here we are, the lessons we learn.

A dance with fate, a pie in the sky,
We juggle our plans while the pigeons fly.
The rubber chicken waits in the wings,
For moments of joy that absurdity brings.

With mismatched shoes and humor bold,
The map to success is rarely sold.
We nod our heads, we scratch our chins,
Through jokes and jests, the fun begins.

So here's to the chaos, a colorful spree,
A riddle disguised as a grand cup of tea.
Laugh at the bumps, let the giggles flow,
For in this wild ride, we truly grow.

The Veiled Horizon

A horizon shrouded in foggy cheer,
With mystery hats made of gummy bears.
What's under the cloak? A dancing clown?
Or perhaps just a scholar with a frown?

We search for signs, for fortune or fate,
As pineapples sashay on the garden gate.
The crystal ball rolls, it's quite out of touch,
Saying, 'Why not try twirls? They're fun, not too much!'

A treasure map drawn by a toddler's hand,
Leading to where the unicorns stand.
With each twist and turn, you'll likely find,
A slice of regret in the pie of the mind.

So lift your cup full of fizzy delight,
And toast to the veil that shimmers so bright.
For beneath all the laughter and silly delight,
Lie secrets that wink, just out of your sight.

The Ripple of Intent

With every thought, a pebble in pond,
The cat's wearing socks, and the dog's quite fond.
A ripple of giggles sails across the way,
As plans trip and tumble, like a ballet.

Intentions float like a balloon in the air,
But pop! There's a squirrel with a very strong glare.
We scribble our dreams on a napkin neat,
As the waitress snickers at our special feat.

Like juggling bananas, we laugh and we try,
To catch life's lemons as they simply fly by.
Each twist and tease, a palette of glee,
Painting our struggles, a laughable spree.

So here's to the ripples that dance and spin,
And to those pesky problems that wiggle on in.
Keep chortling loudly, let joy be your friend,
For in the wild waves, the laughter won't end.

Chasing Shadows

In the light of day, we run from the trees,
Chasing shadows like they all have degrees.
They dart and they giggle, sneaky and sly,
As we stomp and lurk, wondering why.

The sun plays tricks, it's all in good fun,
With shadows that stretch, then twirl and run.
We leap and we bound, our feet in a race,
To catch those reflectors who never leave space.

A tickle of sunlight, a dash of the breeze,
The shadows just laugh, 'Oh, if you please!'
With each little fumble, a grin's just about,
For in this mad chase, a chuckle's allowed.

So next time you wander where shadows take flight,
Join in the game, it'll feel just right.
For hidden in laughter, in jests that abound,
Are whispers of wisdom that dance all around.

A Tidal Wave of Questions

Why's the sky so blue and bright?
Do fish ever get a fright?
Do cats think they are on a spree,
And dogs plotting a grand decree?

Cookies crumble, oh what a mess!
Why's this chaos such a fest?
If socks vanish, what does that mean?
A secret dance? A laundry scene?

Do clouds munch on fluffy pies?
Or just float by, oh, what a surprise!
Is the moon just a giant's cheese?
We laugh, we wonder, hearts put at ease.

So let us swim in this sea of doubt,
With giggles and thoughts, let's twist and shout!
For in this whirlpool, we find the glee,
That questions make life as fun as can be!

The Keys to the Unknown

What's behind that creaky door?
Maybe a dog or a lion's roar!
If keys could talk, what tales they'd tell,
Of hidden treasures and wishing wells!

Do hats have secrets? I must inquire,
Perhaps they hold dreams, or a cosmic fire!
If shoes could walk, would they take a stroll?
To places where we'd reach our goal?

The map's all tangled, the compass spins,
Is it the end, or just where it begins?
Let's grab our lanterns, shine hopeful light,
On the keys that make the unknown bright!

For in the mystery lies the fun,
With a wink and a giggle, yet to be done!
So where to next? We laugh and explore,
With keys to the unknown, what's behind the next door?

The Museum of Moments

Welcome, dear friend, to this quirky place,
With laughter and joy, it's a curious space!
You'll find snapshots of fun all around,
From slips on the ice to wild jumping sound!

There's a corner where laughter's on display,
And stuffed animals join in the play!
With memories hung like colorful art,
Each one a treasure, a tickle to heart!

Old hats that were worn at a magical show,
And rubber ducks from the bath long ago!
Each moment's a gem, a sparkle, a shine,
In this wonderful museum, let's drink some fine wine!

So gather your friends and explore every room,
Laughing at moments that once made us bloom!
In the museum where giggles abide,
Let's cherish each second, and take it in stride!

The Web of Intrigue

In a web spun tight, what secrets lurk?
Do spiders play tricks or just go berserk?
With each little thread, stories unite,
Of fuzzy flies caught in the night!

What if the moon's just a giant's design,
And stars are just sparkles from a big divine?
Do whispers of shadows hide a surprise,
Or just tickle our ears, to make us wise?

With winks from the wind, we giggle and sigh,
What's wrapped in the webs that drift by?
Are mushrooms just umbrellas for thoughts of the night,
Or secret invitations to dance in moonlight?

So let's twirl and spin in this tangled delight,
Where questions are endless, and pondering's bright!
In webs of intrigue, we laugh and we play,
Finding silly wonders in every single way!

Searching for the Light

In the fridge, I seek my fate,
Where the leftover pizza waits.
A slice of joy, a cheesy treat,
Illuminates my evening feat.

I search the shadows, darting quick,
Chasing after a ghostly tick.
Is it purpose or just a snack,
A mystery on my mental track?

With every bite, the questions grow,
Like socks that vanish in the flow.
Do I munch for wisdom or delight?
Beats me—pass the dip tonight!

In this quest that's laid with cheer,
I find my joy, that's crystal clear.
The light I seek is plain to see,
It's really where the snacks will be!

The Riddle in Reflection

Staring hard into the glass,
Where's my mind? A riddle's class.
I puzzle over a sock amiss,
And wonder where my last 'yes' is.

Am I a sage or just confused?
Too many thoughts, all misused.
Perhaps I'm a culinary ace,
Making toast in my own space.

In my reflection, a giggle stirs,
For every thought, a sideways blur.
Is this wisdom or just a jest?
The mirror laughs—'You're just a pest!'

Yet in this chaos, I find a spark,
Between the bites and giggles, a lark.
In each silly thought, I can see,
A riddle wrapped in my mystery.

Veils of Understanding

Beneath each layer, truths reside,
Like homework I no longer hide.
As I peel back life's grand design,
I find I'm lost—did I dine fine?

In recipes of thought I tread,
Mixing joy with things unsaid.
Is clarity a cup of tea?
Or just confusion served with glee?

With every veil, a laugh erupts,
What is this dish? It interrupts.
Understanding is a potluck feast,
Where nothing's right, but all's increased.

So I'll wear my apron with pride,
For life's a kitchen where we bide.
Among the chaos, I'll dance and sway,
Finding meaning, in a funny way.

Unraveling the Threads

Tangled yarn, oh what a plight,
It mocks my plans both day and night.
Each knot I face, a riddle too,
Am I a knitter or just askew?

As I tug on these strings so tight,
A puppet show comes into sight.
Do I control, or do I play?
My life's a stage in disarray.

With every twist, a chuckle sounds,
Seeking answers where none abounds.
Is purpose just a fashion trend?
Or something deeper, around the bend?

Yet here I sit, threads everywhere,
Laughing at the cosmic dare.
In unraveling, I'll find my clue,
Maybe it's just a view askew!

A Dance of Paradoxes

In the circus of dreams, we twirl,
Chasing clouds with a giggle and whirl.
The cat chases tails in a conundrum,
While we search for reason, all numb.

An octopus wears a monocle quite proud,
Reciting Shakespeare to a confused crowd.
What's straightforward is upside-down,
And a frown makes the sun wear a crown.

With socks on our hands, we argue for fun,
Debating if rainbows have a favorite sun.
The punchline hides in a chocolate cake,
As we wrestle with choices we barely make.

So let's dance in our peculiar shoes,
And celebrate all the odd little clues.
In this riddle, we shall find delight,
Laughing at mysteries day and night.

The Jigsaw of Paths

I took a fork in the road today,
A squirrel gave directions, then ran away.
Each piece I find has a quirky twist,
Like macaroni shaped like a fist.

There's a sign that points to Neverland,
But Peter's only selling ice cream by hand.
An owl in glasses announces the way,
While a turtle insists, 'Not today!'.

Puzzle pieces shaped like shoes and glue,
Seem to tell me what I ought to do.
Yet every time I think I have a clue,
I end up knitting a scarf for a bird or two.

But hey, isn't that the fun of the chase?
Like a sunbeam trying to win a race.
The jigsaw may fit or it may not,
And I'll laugh at the mess that I've got.

Unsolved Labyrinths

In a maze where the hedges have grown too high,
I found a lost sock and a curious pie.
Each corner I turn brings a puzzled face,
The walls whisper jokes as I quicken my pace.

I met a rabbit, dressed sharp in a suit,
Debating with shadows about the next route.
He said, 'If you're lost, just stand on one leg!'
And balance while dancing like a seaweed egg.

The minotaur's grip is just a tight hug,
While I untangle thoughts like a snuggly rug.
The answer lies somewhere, maybe near,
But only if you tickle the air with cheer.

So skip through the paths, make a new friend,
In this labyrinth, every turn is pretend.
For the prize is a giggle, not always a win,
Just don't forget to let the silliness in!

The Kites of Thought

Up in the sky, my worries take flight,
My kite's shaped like a cat, oh what a sight!
It loops and it twirls, chasing clouds in a race,
Yelling, 'Catch me if you can' with a silly face.

I ponder the meaning of this breezy chase,
While my sandwich levitates with magical grace.
Thoughts tangled like strings in a wild afternoon,
And a butterfly answers in a funny tune.

A lollipop tree stands tall with delight,
As I giggle at shadows that dance in the light.
What if my dreams were just tricks of the sun?
Swirls of a riddle, all meant for fun.

So let the kites flutter, let the breeze laugh,
Let's find the joy in each quirky half.
For in the whirl of the sky and the glee,
We'll craft our own riddle, just you and me.

The Tapestry of Fate

In a world of quirky threads,
We weave our tales, like clumsy dreads.
With laughter loud, and a wink of fate,
We trip on dreams, yet think it great.

Each stitch a mystery, each knot a tease,
We dance in circles, with jest and ease.
The brighter the yarn, the stranger the plot,
What's woven together, can't be forgot.

Unraveled Veils

Behind each veil lies a riddle,
A snicker, a chuckle, in the middle.
Unfolding surprises, like socks from a bin,
Finding out what's really within.

We juggle our questions, with playful cheer,
Hoping the truths will dance near.
With a twist and a turn, we laugh in delight,
Unraveled veils bring humor to light.

The Contours of Curiosity

Curves and corners of what we seek,
Bump into the sillies, and giggles peak.
With every question, a chuckle ensues,
For answers often wear mismatched shoes.

Poking at puzzles, we poke at life,
With forks and spoons and a hint of strife.
We chase after wisdom, with a clumsy sprint,
Quirky, perplexed, with a playful hint.

Enigmatic Embraces

We hug our dilemmas, with arms open wide,
Wearing smiles even when we slide.
With each embrace, a riddle spins,
Together we laugh at the mess that begins.

Mysterious hugs, tangled in glee,
Whispering secrets, 'What could it be?'
In the jigsaw of jests, we find our own way,
In the grand game, we simply play.

A Symphony of Questions

Why do ducks quack and squirrels dance,
While we ponder our fate, in a comical trance?
Do socks lose their partners to secretive lands,
Or is it all part of life's hidden plans?

Is the moon really cheese, or does it just glow?
With riddles like this, where do we go?
Is laughter the answer, or just a decoy,
That leads us through life with whimsical joy?

Are the stars just old lamps, forgetting to shine,
Or wishes escaping from dreamers like wine?
Each giggle a clue, in the great cosmic play,
Revealing the mysteries in their quirky way.

So let's dance with the doubt, in our wiggly shoes,
With questions that tickle, and silly ol' news.
For in every jest lies a secret embraced,
A clue to the journey, for all of us traced.

The Intrigue of Our Pathways

Do cats plot their moves in a deep, secret lair,
While we fumble about with our messy hair?
Are we merely the jesters, in a grand, silly tale,
Searching for meaning, but missing the sail?

What if clouds are just fluff from the universe's sneeze?
And every line we ponder is made for a tease?
Like trying to find Waldo in an altered dimension,
Where questions are riddled with odd apprehension.

Is breakfast a ritual or merely a snack,
In the cosmic show where conspiracies stack?
Perhaps we're just players in this zany bazaar,
Chasing after answers that flirt from afar.

Yet through the confusion, we stomp and we grin,
Wading through chuckles, let the fun begin.
For as we unravel this colorful thread,
We discover the laughter that dances ahead.

Signs Beneath the Surface

Are rainbows' end points a scam for us all?
With pots of gold, yet we trip and we fall?
What if the fish down below wear top hats,
In a world that spins, filled with curious chats?

Do trees gossip about how the wind loves to play,
While shadows conspire in a sneaky ballet?
Each ripple a whisper, each breeze a sly wink,
As we wander through puzzles, with ink in our blink.

Why do we clutch onto answers like gold,
When the joy is in finding what can't be controlled?
With signs in the underbrush, all out of sync,
We laugh at the mystery, and pause to think.

So let's tiptoe through riddles, and wear silly hats,
For in every odd corner, we're bound to find chats.
And if we look closely, beneath every curve,
We might just discover the joy we deserve.

The Dance of Uncertainty

Does the universe giggle when stars start to fade,
Or is it just playing a cosmic charade?
As we stumble and twirl through the hints and the plays,
We may just be actors in a slapstick ballet.

Why do we worry about each little choice,
When the universe croons in a booming, loud voice?
Should we take the left path or the right one instead,
When both could lead to a clatter of dread?

Is the fish on a bicycle a wise sage, you think?
Teaching us lessons we've yet to ink?
As we skip through the maybes and twiddle our thumbs,
We find that the humor in chaos just hums.

So come join the fray, let's twirl through the jest,
For in every wrong turn, lies a quirky request.
With uncertainty dancing, let's laugh out loud,
In the theater of life, we'll forever be proud.

The Hidden Threads of Fate

In whispers soft, the threads are spun,
A cat's meow, a race to run.
A shoe untied, oh what a sight,
Is this the way to find the light?

We dance to tunes of chance and cheer,
While missing socks seem to appear.
A leaf falls low, a bird takes flight,
Should I bring snacks to this delight?

We laugh and trip on paths unknown,
With riddles that we've never shown.
What's next, a dance with kitchen spoons?
Or finding treasure under moons?

So raise a glass to fate's wild spin,
For in this mess, we find our win.
A puzzle wrapped in layers bright,
Let's skip and hop, it feels just right!

Beneath the Surface of Time

Tick tock, the clock plays games,
With silly jokes and funny names.
A turtle wins the race, so slow,
While we all wonder where to go.

Beneath each tick, a story hides,
Of ice cream trucks and roller rides.
Each moment is a page to turn,
Are we just waiting for a burn?

A jester laughs, the time does fly,
What's on the menu for tonight's pie?
Adventure calls with foamy drinks,
And hints are scattered like our winks.

So dive right in, don't be a bore,
There's magic woven at the core.
With every laugh, we gain a clue,
In the sandwich shop that's calling you!

Echoes of the Unseen Path

Along the path where giggles grow,
A treasure hunt where no one knows.
A sock, a shoe, a wild balloon,
Echoes of laughter fill the room.

With every step, the wisdom leaps,
A puzzle piece that prance and peeps.
Do ducks have dreams of flying high?
Or do they simply paddle by?

A map of crayons leads the way,
To chocolate rivers where we'll play.
Searching for clues in cake and pie,
Who knew that baking would leave us shy?

So grab your pals and make a break,
Let intuition guide the flake.
For echoes linger in the air,
As we all join this light affair!

Journeys Through the Unknown

With backpacks wide, we roam about,
On quests to find what life's about.
We stumble on a puddle's sheen,
And wonder why we've never seen.

The world's a stage, with players bold,
Where jokes are traded, laughter told.
From castles high to valleys low,
It's cosmic play, we steal the show.

A squirrel shares secrets, wise and grand,
While pizza dreams meet jellybean land.
With every step, our hearts will race,
As we trip through this hilarious chase.

So wander on, oh merry crew,
For in the nonsense, we find the true.
Adventure waits, so off we go,
To seek the quirks the world will show!

A Horizon of Hints

In the land of tippy-toes, we dance with glee,
Chasing shadows of answers like a bumblebee.
What's the point, the plan, the grand old scheme?
Just grab a snack and join the team!

We pull the strings of fate like playful cats,
Ponder deep questions while wearing silly hats.
A treasure map? Nay, a book of puns!
The quest for wisdom? Oh, what fun!

We play hopscotch on a road of stars,
While questioning if we're Martians or just cars.
With giggles and whispers, we chase the light,
As purpose hides from us, a playful sight.

So come, dear friend, let's laugh and leap,
Through fields of riddles, our secrets we'll keep.
For in jest and humor, we often find,
The quirkiest paths of the wandering mind.

The Mystical Mosaic

A puzzle with pieces that don't quite fit,
We search for the corner, but it's just a bit.
With mismatched socks and a banana phone,
We question the meaning while sitting alone.

A riddle, a riddle, it dances away,
Like a squirrel on roller skates, come what may!
With every wrong turn, we craft a new tale,
Who knew that the goat could send us to sail?

Painted in colors so wild and bright,
We ponder the stars while taking a bite.
Pizza's the answer? Maybe it's true,
Or perhaps it's the cat that plays peekaboo.

So gather your thoughts, let's scatter them wide,
In the whimsical garden where giggles reside.
The mosaic's unfinished, it shifts and it swirls,
But isn't it better when twirled with some whirls?

The Compass of the Heart

A compass that spins like a cat on a floor,
Points all around, but not to the score.
With hearts shaped like donuts, we chart a new course,
Mixing joy with confusion, like salad with horse.

A map made of jellybeans and clouds,
We follow the laughter, gathering crowds.
"What's the plan?" you ask with a curious face,
"Just dance through the chaos—it's a magical race!"

With each wrong direction, we break into song,
Finding wisdom in giggles, where we all belong.
So let's twirl our compasses, round and around,
And discover the treasures in laughter profound.

For in the wacky wilds of the human heart,
We learn that together, we're never apart.
The compass may spin, but we'll always steer,
With a wink and a chuckle, let's face the frontier!

Whimsy Amongst the Weary

Amidst the bustle and hum of the day,
We find silly moments that drift us away.
A rubber chicken parade in the park,
As the serious folks stare, quite in the dark.

The clock ticks with gusto, but we take a pause,
To chase after bubbles and give them applause.
"What's it all mean?" someone mumbles with glee,
"Perhaps it's to giggle and dance under trees!"

We wear shoes on our heads and frowns on our feet,
Proclaiming that laughter is really the treat.
So gather your burdens; toss them aside,
And ride the fun wave, your inner child's guide.

In whimsy, we find startling delight,
As absurdity dances and twirls in the night.
So here's to the weary; let's twirl through the strife,
For the joy's in the journey, not a map of our life.

A Maze of Choices

In a world of paths that twist and turn,
I ponder choices I might discern.
With each fork, I scratch my head,
Did I choose pizza over bread?

Should I dance or sit and stew?
My socks may clash, but oh, they're blue!
I flip a coin, it lands, oh dear,
I guess it's time for more root beer!

Every alley is a treasure trove,
Yet I find myself in places I've roved.
Am I lost or just exploring?
In this maze, it's laughter I'm storing.

So when in doubt, just take a leap,
The answers here are far from deep.
Embrace the chaos, have some fun,
For every riddle, there's a pun!

Symbols in Silence

In hushed whispers of what's to be,
I decipher symbols like a bee.
An arrow points toward a sunny spot,
But wait, is it 'go' or 'do not trot'?

The cat nods while sipping tea,
What could his paw-sitive vibes decree?
An upside-down smile could mean delight,
Or maybe a catnap, out of sight!

A clock ticks on without a sound,
Does it signal where dreams abound?
I scribble notes, but lose the plot,
Are these the symbols I really sought?

In silence, laughter starts to bloom,
Possibilities fill the room.
Reading signs with silly glee,
Unlocking mysteries, just let it be!

The Story Yet Untold

In every corner, tales unfold,
Some are timid, others bold.
A chicken crossed, but why, oh why?
To chase a nugget in the sky?

Once upon a time, a sock went rogue,
It rebelled against the laundry's vogue.
With a wink, it danced away,
Leaving behind a lonely stray.

There's a fish who dreams of flight,
Swimming high with all its might.
But bubbles burst with every dive,
Is it best to stay alive?

The pages turn with every chuckle,
Creating tales that make me buckle.
The stories wait, a joyful scheme,
It's all just one big, silly dream!

Unfolding the Layers

Peeling back the layers wide,
I find surprises I can't abide.
An onion's tear, a joke it seems,
Each slice reveals my wacky dreams.

Beneath the crust of a pizza pie,
Lies cheesy motives, oh my, oh my!
Toppings scatter, create a mess,
But oh, what fun in this zany quest!

Life's like an onion, or maybe cake,
A slice of humor is what we make.
With each layer comes a twist,
And sometimes, you just can't resist!

So let's unwrap, and not despair,
For laughter hides in every layer.
In this journey, take a chance,
And don't forget to laugh and dance!

Illusions of the Soul's Desire

Like pizza dreams with toppings rare,
We chase the cheese that's floating there.
A wink from fate, a joke from time,
We stir our thoughts, a comic rhyme.

Chasing shadows, we laugh and spin,
Wishing for gold while collecting tin.
With every twist, a punchline laid,
In search of truth, we jest, we're played.

What do we seek, a crown or a shoe?
Life's just a game, but who's got the cue?
The mirror cracks with a smiling face,
A riddle wrapped in a silly embrace.

The Unanswered Questions We Carry

What's in the fridge? Is it still good?
Should I eat it now or wait, I should?
Questions swirl like a pie in the sky,
Topped with laughter, oh my, oh my!

If socks get lost, do they form a crew?
Or dance in circles till we find two?
Tick-tock goes the clock, what's the rush?
Maybe it's time for a cozy hush.

Hidden truths are like cat memes grand,
Fleeting and funny, just out of hand.
The louder you think, the quieter it gets,
A circus of thoughts with no real bets.

A Dance of Questions and Answers

In a ballroom of queries, we twirl and sway,
With answers cheeky, led astray.
The tango of thought, so light and breezy,
Yet sometimes the truth can feel quite cheesy.

"Why is the sky blue?" I ask without pause,
The stars just chuckle, they've seen worse flaws.
A pirouette here, a giggle there,
Our minds are a dance, do we even care?

With questions like confetti, we spread the cheer,
Each answer slips by, but draws us near.
In this playful waltz, we twist and shout,
The punchline's hiding, but we're still out.

The Labyrinth of Tomorrow

Wander through the maze of what might be,
Where every turn yields a new decree.
With signs that giggle, and walls that tease,
Finding the way brings both joy and unease.

The future's a prankster, dressed in a guise,
With bananas slipping and clever lies.
"Left or right?" we ask in jest,
Yet paths of laughter are truly the best.

So here we stand, in a jigsaw of glee,
Mapping the unknown, wild and free.
With each wrong turn, we burst into song,
In the labyrinth of hope, we all belong.

Canvas of Uncharted Thoughts

In a world where socks go missing,
I ponder why my plants keep hissing.
Do they dream of being trees so grand?
Or wish for sunshine on their leafy strand?

Why do cats sit like they own the place?
And why does my mirror show a tired face?
Answers hidden, like the remote control,
I laugh at mysteries that take their toll.

Tangled webs of unasked questions,
Like a jigsaw with skipped directions.
Step right up, join the confounding dance,
Where pondering's sly gaze suggests a chance!

With each odd thought, the canvas grows,
Pulsing with whims only laughter knows.
Carefree brushstrokes fill the open space,
In this world of quirks, we're all a part of the chase.

The Art of Finding Clarity.

In a coffee cup, I seek my muse,
But all I find is last night's snooze.
Why do spoons like to hide away?
And pillows conspire to ruin my day?

When the toaster pops, do I cheer or groan?
It's a golden crust making breakfast known.
Baffled, I sip on another brew,
Hoping it'll trigger an epiphany or two.

Do plants have secrets they never share?
Like where they were before they came to my care?
I chalk it up to metaphysical play,
And giggle as my cat starts to sway.

Searching for answers in a cereal bowl,
Maybe it's true, warmth feeds the soul.
With laughter the brush, here's what I see,
The art of questions is truly the key!

Whispers of Existence

I heard a whisper from my shoe,
It said, 'Hey buddy, what's wrong with you?'
Why do we step on Lego bricks at night?
Is it a test of endurance or fight?

Clouds float by with a knowing grin,
Maybe they know where we've been.
Seagulls cackle while diving for fries,
With wisdom hidden in raucous cries.

A balloon floats high, teasing my hand,
'Catch me if you can!' it says, oh so grand.
While I chase it, I trip on a rug,
Finding joy in the tumble and the shrug.

Quick glimpses of truths dart around,
Like rabbits scurrying on common ground.
Laughing softly at existence's scheme,
I treasure the whispers as part of the dream.

The Puzzle of Tomorrow

Tomorrow's like a game of charades,
As I try to decode the masquerade.
Why do we fumble when plans go askew?
It's like trying to read a menu in a zoo!

The clock's ticking louder, a comic beat,
I trip on my shoelace, oh isn't life sweet?
Can days be boxed like toys on a shelf?
Or are we just jigsaw pieces of ourselves?

Querying fate, I ask with a grin,
Does the spoon have a clue where we've been?
Its silence speaks volumes, I laugh at the game,
The puzzle of future doesn't feel quite the same.

With each twist and turn, the humor reveals,
That falling and laughing are how it conceals.
So here's to the riddles and fun-filled plays,
Tomorrow unfolds in the quirkiest ways!

Reflecting on Reflections

In the mirror, I see my face,
But who's that fool? It's quite a race.
Chasing dreams, I trip and fall,
Is it a voyage or a carnival ball?

Laughter echoes in my own brain,
As thoughts collide like a runaway train.
What's the point of all this fun?
To laugh at shadows when day is done?

In searching for meaning, I lose my way,
Like a cat chasing dust on a sunny day.
The clues are hidden in a cupcake's sprout,
Do I stay lost, or am I not? Shout!

With every answer, more questions arise,
Am I wise or just thinly disguised?
So let's dance to this puzzling tune,
And maybe find sense under a cartoon moon.

The Garden of Forked Paths

In a garden where paths twist and twirl,
I ask a snail, 'What's your big whirl?'
He shrugs and munches on a leaf,
'Guess we're just lost, but isn't it brief?'

Bumping into choices like jellybeans,
Each one sweeter, bursting at the seams.
Do I pick purple, or maybe the green?
Oh wait, what's that? A chocolate scene!

Two roads diverged in a field of grass,
I chose the one that looked like sass.
A penguin strolls, wearing a tie,
'Join the party, mate, don't be shy!'

With giggles and winks, we wander anew,
Each footstep's a chance for something askew.
Life's a maze, filled with silly delight,
So let's skip through it, 'til the end of night.

A Map of Mysteries

I found a map marked with Xs and sighs,
Led to treasure hidden 'neath cloudy skies.
With a compass spun by a cheeky raccoon,
I stumble and tumble, muttering tunes.

The first clue's a riddle, wrapped in confusion,
Is it puzzling fun or just a delusion?
Every corner I turn brings a new surprise,
Like spotting a pig with a pair of new ties.

A treasure chest filled with socks and bad jokes,
I start to wonder if I'm just one of the folks.
What's gold, what's wisdom? I can't seem to sort,
The answers are stuck in a quirky report!

So here's to the journeys that lead us astray,
With laughter and maybe a nap on the way.
Who needs a map when the vibes are so right?
Let's treasure each lost moment in the moon's light!

Chronicles of the Unfathomable

Once upon a riddle, in a land of quirky,
Where wisdom wore socks that were ruffled and murky.
I met a wise owl who danced with a fox,
Together they pondered the mysteries of clocks.

As I sipped on tea brewed from old dusty books,
They told me tales with exaggerated hooks.
'What's the meaning?' I ask with a grin,
They chuckle and say, 'It's just where we've been!'

Chasing the tales that float in the breeze,
We trip on our thoughts like a dance with no keys.
The chronicles flicker like stars in the night,
Do we need to decode? Or just bask in the light?

So here's to the stories, both silly and grand,
To the riddles that slip like sand through our hands.
In the realm of the strange, let's twirl and unfold,
The essence of living is a mystery retold!

Vignettes of Existence

In a dance of spilled coffee, I ponder,
Why socks go missing, like magic conjured.
Amidst joyful chaos, I search for meaning,
While my cat plots a silent, gleeful scheming.

The mailbox whispers secrets, old and bold,
As I chase the ice cream truck, craving cold.
My dreams ride bicycles, wobbling with glee,
While my ambitions sip tea under a tree.

Funny how time flirts with morning light,
Yet here I am, tripping over delight.
My calendar laughs at my endless delays,
As I count the reasons to seize all my days.

So I wear mismatched shoes just for the thrill,
Chasing my shadows, losing track of the still.
Existence is quirky, a comedian's joke,
In the treasure of chaos, the heart awoke.

Echoes in Eternity

Tick-tock, goes the clock with a wink,
As I ponder the thoughts that dare even think.
Are we just echoes, or sounds without end?
While the toast pops up, my breakfast friend.

The sun plays peek-a-boo behind the clouds,
While I wear the hat of a jester, proud.
Dreams float like balloons tied up with string,
In the garden of nonsense, I joyfully swing.

The cat's in a box, plotting escape,
While I search for my keys—another mishap shape.
With laughter as currency, I trade my woes,
In the marketplace of minutes, anything goes.

Time's a slippery fish that's hard to catch,
In the puddles of moments, I endlessly scratch.
So let's raise a toast to this glorious ride,
With giggles as our compass, let's take it in stride.

The Dot-to-Dot of Life

Connecting the dots on a bland old page,
In a whimsical manner, a childish stage.
Each line may confuse as I wiggle and squiggle,
Curiosity reigns, through giggles I giggle.

Oh, what is the meaning of this quirky maze?
Am I an artist or lost in a daze?
With crayons of chaos, I doodle and dream,
Chasing sunset colors, a candy-like theme.

In the spiral of time, I plot my escape,
Like a giraffe in a hat, with great gift-wrapped drape.
Each twist and turn, a comical spree,
Life's a grand game, let's all shout with glee!

So just grab a pencil, and start with a line,
Embrace the absurd, let your laughter refine.
Draw circles of joy, as the fables unfold,
In the dot-to-dot riddle, strange wonders behold.

The Unseen Choreography

In the dance of the days, I trip and I twirl,
As my thoughts do the cha-cha, their ribbons unfurl.
With clumsy pirouettes in the baking sun,
I laugh at my shoes, they're both left and one.

The universe chuckles, spinning its thread,
While I step on an owl, confused but unled.
What's the rhythm of purpose in this grand waltz?
As I tango with thoughts that just won't halt.

Each step is a question, a skip in the beat,
While the toaster conspired with bread, oh so sweet.
As I juggle my dreams in a circus parade,
Life's unseen choreography, bright messes are made.

So, I'll jive with my troubles, a jester's delight,
In this ridiculous ballet, from morning to night.
With laughter as my partner in this intricate play,
I celebrate the absurd, come what may!

The Quest for Meaning

Why do we chase the wind and rain,
In circles round our little brain?
We ask the moon for advice at night,
But it just shines, with no insight.

We search for treasures in the sand,
While tiny crabs laugh, hand in hand.
The map seems clear, but oh dear friend,
Each step reveals a new bend.

In gardens of thoughts, we often tread,
Planting doubts as we stroke our head.
A sunflower asks, 'What's your big plan?'
I chuckle, 'Just trying to be a good man!'

Then we climb the hills of wisdom's peak,
To find a parrot who's learned to speak.
He squawks, "Your quest is just a ruse!"
"Oh really?" I laugh, "What's there to lose?"

Shadows of Unraveled Dreams

In the attic of thoughts, where dust bunnies play,
Shadows dance cheekily, come what may.
A sock's lost its mate, in a game of chance,
While dreaming of socks that could really enhance!

What's this shadow jumping, twirling about?
Is it wisdom or just an odd clout?
I shout out loud, but no one can hear,
The echoes just giggle, then disappear.

The curtains of doubt sway to and fro,
Inviting wild thoughts, like a circus show.
I ask for direction, an answer's reply,
They point to my cat, who just yawns and sighs.

In this funhouse mirror, all truths distort,
Meaning's a jester, who loves the sport.
We dance with uncertainty, like it's a ball,
With every quick turn, we're laughing at all!

Enigmas of Existence

Why do ducks waddle in such a grand way?
Could they be pondering the meaning of play?
With quacks like riddles, they paddle around,
Teaching philosophers without making a sound.

A frog on a log croaks, 'What's the deal?'
Is it wisdom or just a bizarre meal?
It hops and it jumps, with no fear of fate,
While pondering algae, in a philosophical state.

The stars up above twinkle with glee,
While meteors race, setting thoughts free.
"Do we matter?" I call to the night,
They giggle like kids, then snuff out the light.

In this wacky world, where answers confound,
The quest for the truth just goes round and round.
So I'll dance with the stars and swim with the fish,
In this riddle of life, with a plucky swish!

Whispers in the Twilight

In twilight's embrace, the fireflies glare,
They dance with shadows, without a care.
A squirrel debates, 'Is this tree too high?'
While pondering nuts with a thoughtful sigh.

Ghosts of lost socks tumble in the breeze,
As I chase my thoughts with whimsical ease.
A whisper declares, "Don't take it too fast!"
Yet I trip on my shoelace, and the moment's passed.

In gardens of giggles, where secrets bloom,
I find my thoughts weaving tales with a broom.
The moon stifles laughter, rolling on a beam,
While I juggle my worries, or so it would seem.

As crickets compose an offbeat song,
I ponder on puzzles that seem so wrong.
Then I laugh at the mysteries swirling around,
For in this twilight, joy can be found!

Secrets of the Journey

A squirrel stole my sandwich, oh dear,
I chased him around while my lunch cost a beer.
He scampered with glee, thought he was so wise,
Now I ponder my choices and wonder, what's the prize?

A map with no treasure, just a dot in the sea,
I asked a blind turtle if he would help me.
He blinked and he nodded, with a shrug of his shell,
We laughed at the journey; it's quite hard to tell.

Each twist in the trail seemed more absurd,
Like trying to catch thoughts, or chasing a word.
Yet through all the nonsense, I grooved with the flow,
Finding joy in the madness, so off we did go.

So cheers to the wanderers, the lost and the found,
Whose hearts hum a tune in this whimsical round.
With laughter as guidance, we'll dance on our way,
Embracing the questions, come what may!

The Quest for Meaning

A duck in a tuxedo, looking quite grand,
Asking for answers while sipping on sand.
The scholars debated, with wigs on their heads,
"Should we ask the wise cat or the meatball instead?"

A coffee-fueled robot threw riddles galore,
Claiming the secrets were hidden in snore.
But I fell off my chair, laughing out loud,
What's the point of the quest when we've lost the crowd?

The moon wore a smile while blushing so bright,
"Let's tango with chaos, and dance through the night!"
And so we embarked on this wild circus show,
Chasing wind with a wink, letting laughter flow.

Life winks from the sidelines, a playful delight,
"Unlocking the riddle, you might need a kite!"
So grab all your friends, and let's elevate,
In the quest for our meaning, we'll be fashionably late.

Echoes of the Unknown

A frog sings a tune from the depths of the bog,
With each croak and each quirk, it's a clear dialogue.
I pondered its wisdom, a philosopher leaping,
Wondering if silence is all that it's keeping.

The clouds were debating, should they rain or not,
While a snail shouted, "Dude, I've forgotten my spot!"
The breeze laughed aloud, twirling round in its play,
Who knew that confusion could brighten the day?

A cactus named Fred offered sage advice,
"Just carve your own path; sometimes it's like dice."
He wore a top hat, all prickles and flair,
With wisdom in jests, it's a heck of a dare!

So here's to the echoes, both silly and deep,
To the laughter that dances, and makes heartbeats leap.
In mysteries woven, let's embrace the jest,
For in humor and joy, we surely are blessed.

The Labyrinth of Dreams

A hamster on wheels, racing round in a spin,
Declared he was seeking the meaning within.
He tripped on a thought, then spun out of sight,
Proclaiming loud, "The answers are light!"

In corners of chaos, where socks often roam,
I found a lost kitten who claimed it was home.
He wore on his collar a sign reading 'wise',
In riddles and giggles, he spun wild replies.

The lanterns were chuckling, flickering bright,
Guide your feet forward, through shadows and light.
With a wink and a nod, the maze came alive,
What if all the puzzling just taught us to thrive?

So let's bounce through the labyrinth, hand in paw,
With silliness guiding, let's take a wild draw.
For dreams are the quirkiest maps we can make,
In the end, it's the laughter that's ours for the take.

The Paradox of Now

In a world so bright, what's next in line?
We search for answers, but they just decline.
Where's the treasure? Is it hid or shown?
Perhaps it's in the pizza that we've grown!

We dodge the clocks with their tick-tock sound,
Yet here we are, spinning round and round.
Our maps are scribbles, our compass a joke,
Was that a breakthrough or just a poke?

Here's a tip: just take out a snack,
Chase the giggles, there's no need to rack.
In every chuckle, a riddle might hide,
As we dance through the nonsense, side by side.

So if you're lost and feeling quite dazed,
Just laugh it off; life's wacky and crazed.
The answer is silly, wrapped in delight,
Now dance with the chaos, or take flight!

Navigating the Uncharted

In waters deep where fish wear hats,
I ponder on why my bread's gone flat.
Star maps look upside down tonight,
Are they guiding me wrong or just shy of light?

With every splash, I learn to swing,
Like birds on bicycles trying to sing.
The compass spins, it knows no rest,
A pinwheel direction? I like that best!

I met a pirate who only eats cake,
He claims it's the secret to life's grand wake.
His parrot squawks riddles, all printed on foam,
Together we sail, but where's now home?

So map your laughter and steer with a grin,
With whims as your wind, let the voyage begin.
And if you stray where logic won't play,
Just wade through the giggles, they'll brighten your day!

Fragments of a Whole

Here I sit with my puzzling crew,
We're maybes and what-ifs, a colorful hue.
Each piece a thought, not a perfect fit,
Yet oddly together, we manage to sit!

I found a sock that was last seen in June,
With a jellybean cat that hums a tune.
Fragments of fortune, confetti of dreams,
Life's a party, or so it seems.

In searching for sense, we've spun quite a tale,
Like a cat in a hat riding a snail.
What's complete? We're not even sure,
Just fret over candy and maybe a lure!

So gather your pieces, don shiny parade,
In laughter and chaos, we've unmade the blade.
For in every fragment and chuckle we share,
There lies a whole that's beyond compare!

The Hidden Accord

Beneath the chaos, agreements are found,
Like squirrels debating how to jump around.
In the midst of the madness, there's rhythm, you see,
Even the waffles are jamming with glee!

The cuckoo's laughing, the sun gives a sigh,
As shoes become hats, and we all wonder why.
Underneath it all, there's a dance on the floor,
As we skip through the banana peels, wanting more!

When serious whispers try to steal the show,
I suggest we all wear socks made of snow.
For the hidden accord is a chuckle and wiggle,
In sync with the wobbly, we laugh 'til we giggle.

So clap your hands and shake like a tree,
In the opera of nonsense, be wild and be free.
The world's absurdity, a sweet masquerade,
Join the revelry — let your spirit parade!

The Puzzle of Being

In a box of socks, I found my fate,
The cat just laughed; was it a date?
With pieces missing, I pondered long,
Is harmony just a silly song?

A missing lid on my coffee cup,
Sipping thoughts from the bottom up.
Do I need answers or just some fun?
Maybe the puzzle is just to run!

I asked the owl perched on a tree,
"Is the riddle just silly, like this tea?"
He hooted back with a wink and nod,
"Sometimes a question is just a plod!"

So I dance with shadows, chase my tail,
In this grand maze where clues set sail.
Each twist and turn, a laugh or two,
Perhaps the answer is in the stew!

Secrets of the Heart's Compass

A map drawn in crayon, all colors bright,
Leads me in circles by day and night.
The North says 'left', while the South yells 'right',
Guess who got lost in the morning light?

My compass spins like a whirling dervish,
Pointing to tacos, in search of perish.
Is it Santorini or a taco stand?
Maybe the secret is in the unplanned.

I asked the stars, sparkling above,
"Is finding you a game of shove?"
They twinkled back, with laughter so light,
"Just dance around, you'll be alright!"

So here I wander, with giggles and sighs,
Chasing the whimsy of time's great surprise.
With each wrong turn, I find a new laugh,
Maybe the joy is the secret path!

Reflections in a Glassy Stream

In a pond so shiny, I take a peek,
My reflection waves back; is it me I seek?
The frog serenades, but I'm tone-deaf,
Singing of dreams that are far from theft.

The water ripples with guffaws galore,
Circles of laughter, forever explore.
Do fish have musings, or just swim away?
What's the point? Let's just splash and play!

They say the truth lies beneath the surface,
But the ducks quack louder, not so earnest.
I ponder deep thoughts, then slip and fall,
Just a splash of giggles is the best of all!

So I wade in the stream, making goofy faces,
In this dance of reflections and silly places.
Each bubble that pops is a riddle undone,
In this watery mess, I've already won!

The Maze of Our Stories

A labyrinth made of socks and cheese,
Winding and twisting with graceful ease.
Where's the exit or is it a joke?
With every turn, another poke!

Wandered through tales of purple and green,
Chasing the laughter, a curious scene.
Do words have legs, or do they just run?
Maybe the fun is just never done!

A chicken crossed paths with a dancing bear,
They exchanged stories, and no one cared.
The path led to laughter, a treasure chest,
Filled with zany tales; I was truly blessed!

So here's to the maze, so odd but bright,
With twists and turns that tickle the night.
Each lost step a giggle, each stumble a cheer,
Let's keep wandering; there's magic here!

The Weaving of Hopes and Fears

In a loom where dreams often fray,
A cat naps around, stealing the day.
Colors clash in a playful spree,
A tapestry laughs—what could it be?

Threads that shimmer, and some that snag,
Woven patterns in an old grocery bag.
Each stitch whispers of what might come,
While I sip my tea, oh so glum!

Patterns twist, oh, what a dance!
One thread's a goldfish in a trance.
The more I ponder, the less I know,
Until the cat gives a sly little show.

Each thread a question—what's the score?
As the shadows gather, I search for more.
Finding laughter in every twist and turn,
In this crazy quilt, I take my turn!

In Search of the Unsung Truth

With a magnifying glass, I roam the halls,
Looking for nuggets past magical walls.
The mysteries dance in a dizzying way,
Like socks that vanish on laundry day.

They say the truth is a slippery fish,
But I'm more concerned about my lunch dish.
Is it nestled in leftovers or under the bed?
Maybe it's hiding right under my head!

Gnomes in the garden make perfect sense,
While searching for answers grows quite immense.
The squirrels nod knowingly—don't be a fool!
They hide nuts, not truths in a magical pool!

So here I sit, scratching my chin,
As the secrets swirl and the laughter begins.
Twirling in circles, I spot something askew,
Is that the truth? Oh wait, it's my shoe!

Threads of Destiny Knotted Tight

In a world spun with yarns of delight,
I trip over destiny, oh what a sight!
A tug here, a pull there, oh my, oh dear,
Seems my fate's tangled with last year's veneer.

Dancing in circles, I wrestle the fate,
A cat plays poker, isn't it great?
The threads twist and turn, they love to conspire,
While I search for meaning amidst this quagmire.

With each knot that I tie, I giggle and sigh,
Can't a person just wander and fly?
Yet here in this chaos, what can I find?
Laughter and mayhem are perfectly aligned!

So I'm here with my yarn, pulling with glee,
The more I unravel, the funnier me.
Life's threads all fray; it's all come undone,
In this crazy cosmos, I'm just having fun!

The Scribe of Silent Motions

In a quiet corner, the scribe takes aim,
Writing stories of whispers, never the same.
A blank page waits, so patient and prim,
While the shenanigans sparkle like a whimsical whim.

Each heartbeat a secret, each blink a rhyme,
Traipsing through moments as I sip my lime.
Jotting down laughter, the joy, the dismay,
In the grand circus, it's all just play.

The walls giggle softly, the chairs sway to tune,
As I pen down the nonsense beneath the moon.
A dance of the fleeting, captured so sly,
In this silent commotion, the absurdities fly!

Here's to the scribbles that lead us astray,
To the funny little truths that come out to play.
A story unwritten, a life often planned,
In the dance of the scribes, we just take a stand!

The Essence of the Uncertain

What's the point of socks, we ask,
When one goes missing, it's quite the task.
Hiding in corners, they chuckle and smirk,
While we chase them around, it's quite the perk.

Should we dance with fate or just sit and stew?
Perhaps wear a hat, but whose hat will do?
The cat takes a nap, while we plot and plan,
Maybe it's simple, like, 'Just be a fan.'

Questions whizz by like cars on a track,
And purpose is just a fun little quack.
So we laugh at the road, and we laugh at the strife,
Maybe the joke is just being in life.

Embrace all the chaos, let laughter resound,
For the quirks of existence, they know no bound.
So wear mismatched socks and wiggle your toes,
In the grand game of waiting, it's fun, who knows?

In the Corners of Time

Tick-tock goes the clock, but what does it mean?
Is it the sound of a joke or a routine?
The seconds slip by as we munch on our fries,
Wondering how many naps fit in the skies.

What's hiding in seconds, what's blazing in hours?
A squirrel might know, he collects all the powers.
In the corners of time, do absurd things unfold?
Or just echoes of laughter lost in the cold?

Oh, calendars crinkle, they wrinkle and sigh,
As we scribble our plans that we never comply.
Let's leap into fun and forget about charts,
For the map of our dreams is a work of fine arts.

So let's flaunt our quirks like a badge worn with pride,
In the corners of time, let's go for a ride.
With confetti of moments, we make our own way,
Each blue sky a canvas, happy chaos at play!

The Secret Garden of Purpose

In a garden of thoughts where oddities bloom,
We plant flaky dreams and we water with gloom.
Sprouts of confusion, they poke through the clay,
And we giggle at weeds that dance in the fray.

What's the secret, you ask, as you prune back the doubt?
It's all about joy, let's give a loud shout!
With daisies of laughter and roses of fun,
Who knew gardening puzzled could also be sun?

We chat with our plants, as they sway in the breeze,
"What's the purpose of this?" and they rustle with ease.
A snail shares a tale of a trip gone awry,
While we sip our lemonade under the sky.

So let's cultivate quirks in this wild vibrant space,
As we embrace the absurd and laugh at our pace.
For the blooms might be weird, and the fruit could be strange,
In the secret of purpose, we let the odd change.

Voices from the Abyss

In shadows that giggle, and dark corners hum,
Lurks a chorus of questions, combined into fun.
"Who ate all the snacks? And why is toast great?"
As echoes of laughter, they cook up our fate.

Whispers from nowhere, they coo and they tease,
"What's the meaning of cheese? Is it really to please?"
Insanity's pet goldfish swims round and around,
In the depths of the void, absurd truths abound.

Jokes tossed in the void, they bounce back with flair,
As we juggle our hopes like we just don't care.
"Why not wear a tutu while floating on air?"
As the void cracks a smile, we join in the dare.

So here's to the whispers, the chuckles, the jest,
In the embrace of the quirky, let's give it our best.
For voices from abysses may not hold the key,
But who needs a riddle when you're utterly free?

Fleeting Moments

A squirrel stole my sandwich, quite the thief,
It danced on the lawn, beyond belief.
I wondered if it sought a deeper call,
Or just loved crispy bread—after all!

As I chased the critter, my shoes untied,
I laughed at the riddle, my thoughts unoccupied.
Was that moment meant for profound insight?
Or just for getting crumbs in a giant bite?

The sky turned blue, then suddenly gray,
I pondered why time never seemed to stay.
Did the universe chuckle at my silly chase?
Or simply enjoy my bewildered face?

With laughter echoing in the fading light,
I pondered if squirrels found wisdom in flight.
Each fleeting moment a question, absurd,
In the comedy of chaos, I found my word.

Infinite Questions

Why does my cat stare at the wall so keen?
Does it plot to rule this living screen?
I ask if it's life's great secret exposed,
Or just the echo of dreams it loathed.

I pondered as tea brewed, a ritual lost,
Do biscuits hold answers, or just make us tossed?
For every sip taken, a thought took flight,
Was it wisdom or madness that brought forth the night?

A goldfish swims circles, or is it a maze?
In bubbles it whispers, I'm lost in a daze.
Do mirrors reflect what we really think,
Or just show a face that's void with no link?

In laughter we wander, each question a jest,
To chase the elusive, the quest for the best.
Yet humor writes wisdom, in jest, in delight,
While we tumble and laugh, under stars that ignite.

Traces of the Unexplained

In the attic I found an old sock and a shoe,
Do they plot a great escape, or just hide from view?
A pair once enchanted, now lost to the years,
Are they seekers of purpose, or just lost in fears?

A dusty old book whispers tales of the past,
Do riddles and rhymes hold wisdom to cast?
I flip through the pages, each word leaves a mark,
Yet the answer eludes me, like light in the dark.

A fog creeps in softly, the night's feeling sly,
Will the mysteries fade, or just learn to fly?
With laughter in shadows, I dance with the unknown,
And question if anything's truly my own?

So here's to confusion, to socks gone astray,
To dancing with laughter, and letting it play.
For in every enigma that always remains,
We find traces of humor in all of life's games.

Maps of the Unknown Journey

I crafted a map with crayons and dreams,
To find all the answers, or so it seems.
Marked X on the spot where I stumbled and fell,
Is it treasure or trouble? I can't really tell.

With each twist and turn, my directions go wild,
As I chase after squirrels, you can call me a child.
Will I ever see wisdom on this silly ride?
Or just end up lost in the great boondoggle slide?

The compass spins wildly, a joke of its own,
Am I set for adventure, or just overthrown?
I laugh at the chaos while exploring the map,
Doesn't the journey make sense of the clap?

So here is my quest, with giggles galore,
With each step I take, I discover one more.
In the unknown, the laughter, my heart finds a way,
Mapping fun in the mystery, come what may.

The Imprint of Forgotten Words

I found a note crumpled, lost in my bag,
Did it hold a great truth or just something to brag?
With words all a jumble, like spaghetti on toast,
It begs for attention, while being a ghost.

I scribble my thoughts in ink that won't flow,
Each letter a riddle, each line mighty slow.
Could prose hide a meaning in whimsical cheer?
Or just capture nonsense that no one will hear?

On a napkin, the secrets of tea-stained delight,
Look closely, perhaps you'll uncover the light.
For laughter's the imprint that sticks to our hearts,
While the mystery dances as each word departs.

So here's to the phrases that tickle and tease,
To the nonsense we scribble with effortless ease.
In the laughter we share, in the words that we cast,
Lie answers forgotten, and riddles that last.

The Silent Symphony of Choices

In a dance of plans, we sway so fine,
Every step a puzzle, a twist in the line.
Should I wear blue socks or bright green shoes?
Sometimes it feels like I've got none to choose.

Chasing dreams like cats chasing tails,
With giggles and flops, we weave our tales.
Skip a rock or bake a pie,
Which one gets me a slice of the sky?

The orchestra plays, but no one hears,
Except for squirrels cheering with their peers.
Twirling with snacks, a rare kind of grace,
Who knew confusion could wear such a face?

Thus we stumble, twirl, and prance,
In the waltz of chaos, we take a chance.
With each misstep, laughter thrives,
And in this riddle, our joy survives.

Mysteries Sown in Everyday Moments

A toaster's a riddle, a cryptic device,
Slides bread in, but spits out paradise.
How does it know when the toast's done?
Does it have a clock or just really good fun?

The mailman arrives with letters and glee,
What secrets he carries, oh what could they be?
Is it a message from aliens, clear?
Or just bills and ads that'll pull on my ear?

The coffee pot murmurs in a sleepy light,
Whispers of energy for a glorious flight.
Each sip a journey, a potential spark,
Into the world or just back in the dark?

With cats on the prowl and socks gone astray,
These little oddities brighten the day.
Like treasure maps in bright neon hue,
Imagine the stories, all waiting for you.

The Story Written in Starlight

Stars twinkle like confetti in a bowl,
Mysterious tales they eagerly unroll.
Are they simply baking, just swirling in flight?
Or plotting against us in the cover of night?

Each twinkling spark, a giggle of fate,
Do they bet on my choices and calculate?
With every wish, are they starting a game,
And knowing my secrets, my hopes are the same?

Planets are winks, comets a flurry,
While we spin 'round, oh, in a hurry.
Do they laugh as we argue and ponder our path,
Or is this just cosmic eternal math?

In this grand show, we wink back and forth,
I write my script, a theater's worth.
So grab your popcorn and join the delight,
In the cosmic riddle of this starlit night.

Illuminated Paths and Dark Corners

In the alley of choices, shadows will creep,
But which path to take, oh, that makes me leap!
Should I follow the squirrel or stay by the fence?
In this game of life, I need some good sense!

Bright lights are flashing, like disco in fog,
Do we grin at the melody or trip on the dog?
With each step I take, I consider my fate,
Is it a spin on a wheel or just skipping plates?

Then comes a whisper, a tickle of doubt,
Like when you realize the milk's run out.
Should I make a run, or just play it sly?
Maybe I'll draw a mustache and go try!

In corners of day, where the light barely plays,
I dance with my dreams in whimsical ways.
Through laughter and riddles, I'll find my own score,
And maybe the shadows aren't scary, but more.

The Secret Compass

A compass spins without a clue,
It points to lunch or maybe stew.
With maps that twist and turn askew,
I'm lost, but hey, I've got a view!

The North Star said, 'You should find gold!'
But here I sit, just feeling bold.
A treasure chest that's twenty years old,
Should I dig—or just do what I'm told?

Wanderlust is quite the jest,
Perhaps my couch is simply best.
The path unfolds, a comical quest,
Yet snacks are near, I am obsessed!

So off I go with dreams in tow,
Adventurous- my heart will glow!
But really—who needs a grand show?
A pizza slice is just so pro!

Paths Through the Unseen

On roads where squirrels dance and play,
And shadows hint at a buffet.
With each detour, I sway and sway,
Did I eat lunch, or is it just hay?

Invisible paths twist to the left,
With footsteps of those who just left.
I follow signs through mischievous theft,
The only clue is a candy cleft.

'Why not this way?' a frog does croak,
His wisdom's wrapped in ancient smoke.
Around the bend, I start to choke,
Was that a joke or just a poke?

While plotting routes, my phone goes dead,
Was it a plan or just in my head?
Still, laughter echoes where I tread,
Adventure's fun—grab cookies instead!

Mysteries in the Mist

Fog rolls in with secrets galore,
What's lurking behind that old door?
A raccoon with a taste for s'more,
Or just my spouse, who's been out for a chore?

In swirling gray, I trip and slide,
Was that a ghost or my cat's pride?
With every step, I'm now the guide,
To unknown folds of time, we glide.

Questions rise like dough in a bowl,
What's the purpose? A cosmic role!
Yet laughter bubbles, it's good for the soul,
I'll find my answer—then eat a whole.

Through shadows deep, and twists untold,
I chase the fun, as fortunes unfold.
With every stumble, I'm bought and sold,
The mystery's sweet, like warm bread bold!

The Colors of Ambiguity

A canvas bright, yet I'm not sure,
Is that a fish, or something obscure?
With splashes vibrant, I must endure,
My art's a mess, but hey, it's pure!

Each stroke a giggle, a splatter, a tease,
Blue for the sky, or is it for cheese?
Maybe my brush is a fit for these,
Or just a ploy to bring you to your knees.

What do the colors truly say?
Is yellow a frown, or a sunny day?
With every drip, I'm lost in the fray,
But laughing helps to lighten the gray.

So paint your joy with wild delight,
Smudge the edges, hold on tight!
The hue of chaos feels just right,
In life's grand gallery of the night!

The Journey Inward

In a world of socks and cereal bliss,
I ponder the meaning with a silly twist.
Is it in the fridge or hiding in my shoe?
Perhaps it's in the laughter shared by a few.

I chase my thoughts like a cat with a string,
Dancing and tumbling, oh what joy they bring!
Each question a riddle, wrapped in bold delight,
As I trip over answers that eluded my sight.

With cupcakes and sprinkles, I set forth my quest,
Will I find the mystery hidden in jest?
In doodles and giggles, my heart starts to sing,
Unraveling puzzles, oh what fun they bring!

So here's to the journey, both silly and bright,
As I paint my confusion in laughs and in light.
Though answers may waltz just beyond my reach,
I'll savor each riddle, there's joy in the breach.

The Silent Conversations

I chat with my plants, they nod and they sway,
"What's the secret to flowers?" I casually say.
They whisper in green, a shushing of leaves,
While I sip on my tea and ponder my cleaves.

With each quiet moment, I ask all around,
"Is happiness found where lost socks abound?"
They gurgle a giggle, a rustle in the breeze,
As I scratch my head, aiming to please.

Do ants have a clue or perhaps a parade?
If only they'd chat, no secrets to trade.
I'd strut like a robot, all quirky and free,
As squirrels throw confetti and join in with glee.

But still, I remain with my tea and my thoughts,
In a world that's a puzzle of smiles and knots.
The answers may hide, in the places I don't,
But I'll keep on conversing, in this riddle I won't.

Chasing Fleeting Glimpses

I sprint after shadows like a dog gone awry,
With questions that flutter like butterflies in the sky.
"Is it here or there?" I dash left and right,
In pursuit of a riddle that giggles at night.

The fridge hums its wisdom, the clock ticks in jest,
As I fumble through dreams like a quirky treasure chest.
Each darting reflection, each laugh from the past,
Is it just a mirage? Or something to hold fast?

I chase every moment, a merry-go-round,
With marshmallows and laughter just waiting to be found.

Each blink is a clue, a clue I can't paste,
Yet the joy in the searching, I utterly taste.

So here I keep running, my heart in a race,
For each fleeting glimpse brings a smile to my face.
With the riddles around me, I'll twirl with delight,
Chasing joys that make the mundane feel bright.

Whispered Clues

I found a note stuck to my orange juice cap,
"Seek out the wisdom, don't fall in the trap!"
It tickled my senses, a mystery to mend,
So I laughed with my toast, my bread-shaped friend.

Whispers of giggles float high on the breeze,
"Look underneath the sofa for life's hidden keys!"
With a squint and a wiggle, I dive down below,
To find a gum wrapper and a sock in tow.

The cat gives a smirk, does she know more than me?
With a flick of her tail, she climbs up a tree.
"Hey, what's the punchline?" I shout to the sky,
But the clouds just chuckle, "Oh give it a try!"

So I gather my treasures, in laughter I'm steeped,
For the clues are reminders that joy's often reaped.
In the chaos, I dance, for each riddle and clue,
Paves the way for chuckles and fun times anew.

www.ingramcontent.com/pod-product-compliance
Lightning Source LLC
Chambersburg PA
CBHW072149200426
43209CB00051B/956